GETTING
what
MATTERS

"It's admirable how Anis channels years of experience and learning in deal-making into engaging, easily relatable negotiation stories. *Getting What Matters* is a resource you'll want to keep close at hand, turning to it as you encounter situations similar to those it describes."

— **Alfonso Aranda Arias**,
Cloud Infrastructure and Datacentre Executive

"Anis uses storytelling to dissect and teach highly practical insights on a crucial skill often overlooked in formal education: how to negotiate effectively. I sincerely wish I had this book years earlier, it would have spared me countless struggles in getting what mattered to me."

— **Mark de Stadler**, International Executive Communication Expert, ex Dale Carnegie

GETTING
what
MATTERS

NEGOTIATION STORIES
AND POWERFUL LESSONS TO ACHIEVE
YOUR GOALS WITH ADULTS AND KIDS

ANIS BENNANI

For my mum, my dad, my wife, and
my two little daughters.

CONTENTS

PROLOGUE

WHEN I FINISHED primary school in Morocco, my mum decided that I should go to one of the best private schools for the middle and high school levels so I could have better opportunities in the future. This school was one of the most expensive, and the fee was a financial stretch for my family.

After a year of study, when I had a track record of getting good grades, my mum told the school's owner that I was helping his school's reputation and should be rewarded for that. She got her first discount on the fee.

I was selected to be a member of the Moroccan youth parliament—another discount. I was getting good rankings in a national math Olympiad—another discount.

When I finished middle school and was about to start high school, the fee was still high. The school's owner told my mother that he could not go any lower. She said, "He is really enjoying learning here and he is bringing some good values to your school; how can we keep this going?" He did not budge, so she kept me at home for several weeks after classes began. I didn't know why my mother was doing this or what she had in mind. We can say that she loves taking risks.

She went to see the owner again and told him, "I am about to put him in another school, and he is not very happy about that. We are both losing here. What would you advise?" He lowered the fee again and asked her to bring me back.

In some countries like Morocco, negotiation or haggling is customary; most of the time, you don't expect to pay the sticker price. But what my mum did took this bargaining several levels beyond what many Moroccans would expect, and she did this by understanding what values we were bringing to the table and figuring out the motivation of the other side.

Did I learn from her? Not straight away.

I thought about negotiation as a power game in which I demonstrated that I had the final word. My style was "my way or the highway." My mum was calm, and her manner, soft.

I came to realize that despite her soft manner, she had this insane persistence in coming back to issues until she reached her goals—what mattered to her.

I asked her how she was doing it, but she did not know. It all came naturally to her.

While growing up and then starting my professional career, I became more passionate about negotiation and loved sharing what I learned. As I practiced with the people around me, I started observing that you don't usually get what you deserve, but get what you negotiate.

I was fortunate to land in a career that requires negotiation in the traditional sense, through buying and selling. But we negotiate in many kinds of situations, and the stories in this book reflect that variety. Through my career, I have met a very diverse set of people who do not fit the stereotype of people working in the sales or procurement fields. I started seeing how you can connect with people despite their being very different from you—culturally, socially, whatever type of difference you can imagine.

I was fortunate to have a platform that let me keep testing negotiation concepts so I could keep the most effective ones.

While I was doing this work, something kept striking me again and again in myself and others. I saw people embarking on negotiations, most of the time in a passionate way, and losing their focus on what they needed to achieve at the end—on what really mattered to them. I saw people negotiating very hard for a nice title at work, when what really mattered to them was money. I saw others negotiating with their kids to finish their homework before going to bed, when what really mattered was helping their kids develop a sense of responsibility.

Something else that struck me was that I was spending a lot of effort (mainly through my years in sales) to learn techniques to influence others to do what I wanted.

Through this process, I ended up learning that to influence others, I needed to start first with myself, developing more self-awareness about what I really needed and how I was feeling about a situation before even daring to influence anyone else.

Without this self-awareness, we tend to go back to our default modes of dealing with others—our habitual, automatic behaviors. You might have grown up seeing that intimidating people is the best way to get what you want or that giving up is the easiest way to deal with a conflict. But you don't have to be stuck with the behaviors you've been conditioned to perform or expect. You can learn how to negotiate differently—and more effectively.

So what is this book about?

My aim is to share what I've seen working in real life to help you get what matters to you. You might get more (of whatever you're seeking) or get other people to say yes to you in the process, but the aim is to raise your awareness about getting what matters. I will be sharing these observations through 24 stories.

You will find stories about kids as well. Why is that? I have two young daughters. Most people would say that their kids are the toughest negotiators they've seen, and I don't disagree. I believe it's the parents' duty to teach kids how to get what matters to them, by showing, not just telling.

Most education systems do not prepare us for real-life negotiation situations. While growing up, kids lose their natural ability to engage with others and come closer to what they want. Through the years, kids shift from getting what they want and end up getting just what they were given. They start losing the simple ability to ASK.

I am writing this book for everyone, not for a specific role or function at work or at home. By reading these stories, you will hopefully come to the realization that achieving your goals, the ones that matter most to you, is achievable for everyone and most of the time, whatever you do in life. It takes persistence and practice, trial, and failure.

I suggest that you first read this book as a set of stories, and then pick one story and try to practice its negotiation concept until you become familiar with it. Then go on with another story, and another. The best way to get better is through practice.

I hope you enjoy this book.

PART I

GETTING WHAT MATTERS

1 | WHAT ARE YOU REALLY AFTER? WHAT MATTERS TO YOU?

STORY

Jessica and Imran lived in London. They were getting married soon and were having Jessica's wedding ring made in the Antwerp diamond district in Belgium, as shops in Antwerp were known to provide some of the best diamond rings in Europe. While visiting one of the diamond stores and speaking with Guy, its owner, Jessica and Imran chose a ring design with a specific diamond to be brought from the US. The ring, with the diamond, cost 15,000 euros. Jessica and Imran were supposed to come back in four weeks to pick it up.

Two days before their trip to Antwerp, Guy called Imran, telling him that the diamond delivery from the US would be delayed by one week. He kept pushing his provider in the US for an early delivery, but his provider needed more time to get the right design.

Jessica and Imran were under significant pressure as their wedding was in three weeks and they had only two weekends to finish their preparations. Delaying the trip to Antwerp would affect their other preparations.

Imran got very frustrated. He started shouting at Guy, telling him that he had failed to get them the high-quality ring he had promised. Imran said he would start writing bad reviews of Guy's store all over the internet. Guy was calm initially, but soon got frustrated, too. He felt that he had been let down by his provider and that he was trying his best to find a solution with no success.

Guy kept telling Imran that his shouting was not helpful and that if Imran wanted to cancel the order, Guy could send him back his 10% deposit. Both men started shouting, and Imran finally hung up the phone.

When Jessica learned about the situation, she felt frustrated. Then she decided to call Guy to discuss the matter. Speaking to him, she realized that there might be other options that allowed them to keep their timelines:

1. If they could buy a diamond with slightly better specs, the US provider could get them the new diamond on time. The new one would cost 10% more, but Guy offered to split this extra cost with Jessica and Imran.

2. Jessica and Imran could see if it was possible for them to push their trip out by one week and get other preparations done on the coming weekend.

3. Guy could send the ring to an associate in London. Instead of traveling to Antwerp on one of the two weekends left before their wedding, Jessica and Imran could see this associate in London during the week. Staying in London would allow them to make more progress on their wedding preparations.

DEBRIEF & ADVICE

Imran forgot that his main goal was getting the diamond ring they wanted in time for their wedding. He started shouting at Guy, threatening him, and forgetting that he still needed to deal with him. Imran was very focused on going to Antwerp the next week, considering that trip as his main goal, whereas what really mattered to him was getting a ring that he and Jessica both loved and having it in time for their wedding.

When Jessica got involved, she had their real goal in mind. She figured out that there were at least three ways to get what she and Imran needed, and going to Antwerp on a certain weekend was only one way.

Negotiation is usually defined as "influencing someone else to get what you want." It is a great definition. The issue is that we tend to focus a lot on the "influencing someone else" part and less on the "getting what you want" part.

Let me explain. We try very hard to understand the other side's motivation and state of mind, and we consider what to say, when to say it, how to kick off the discussion, and so on and so forth. The other side, the part not under our control, is unknown, so we put a lot of effort into understanding and influencing that person or company.

Then we tend to skim quickly through the "what we want" part, as it is within ourselves, within our control. We say, "Well, who knows me better than I know myself?" We assume that what we want is what we need, and that what we need is what really matters to us. Often, however, these things—our wants, needs, and most important goals—are different.

Let's say you have a job, and you want a raise because what you *need* is to save more money, because what *matters* to you is having a feeling of security. What *matters* is freedom—not being at the mercy of your job and being able to quit it whenever you want. So you start putting in place all the strategies in the world to convince your boss, the boss of your boss, the friends of your boss, and the best friends of the boss of your boss that you are really worth it and you are the top performer of the year.

If you start a side hustle that generates a good level of monthly income, you can get what matters to you—that blend of security and freedom—and you won't even need to negotiate with your boss.

The starting point of any negotiation is figuring out what really matters to you. Then you can work toward getting it.

Understanding what you are really after is crucial. To uncover this, you can ask two questions:

1. What do I really need?
2. What problem do I need to solve?

We can get easily caught up in a heated conversation and lose sight of what we need to achieve. When this happens, pause and check if what you are doing is helping you getting what matters to you.

Arguing with the other side might be your first reaction when perspectives are different. We might think that giving supportive arguments on why our position is valid is enough to influence the other side, and when this method fails, frustration starts to pile up. It's usually tempting to prove your point and prove the other side wrong.

If you find yourself in a similar situation, nothing prevents you from putting the discussion back on track. You can always explain to the other side that you got emotional—something that nearly everyone will understand—and say that your objective now is to find a solution to the problem.

Going back to Jessica and Imran's situation: When Guy offers to split the 10% difference, should she take this deal or should she push back? My answer is: who cares? She should accept it if it is meeting her goal, or reject it if it is not.

The aim of this book is not to teach you how to split the pie or how to never split the difference in half, or by a quarter or a third. The main aim is to raise your awareness of what really matters to you and then help you keep your focus throughout the negotiation process so you can get it.

You might be thinking, "Oh dear, I bought this book to learn how to be a great deal maker, like Churchill or Henry Kissinger or those who are solving intergalactic conflicts. Here I am reading this story about this couple buying a diamond ring in Belgium." Well, if you can't manage the situations that might appear trivial to you, how can you manage the ones with higher stakes? The negotiation learnings in this book are relevant to the simplest situations as well as to the harder ones.

2 | WHAT MATTERS TO THEM? ASK THEM

STORY

Scott had been asking Jeff, his boss, for a promotion for the past two months. The issue was that Scott was promoted less than a year ago, and company policy is to spend at least 18 months on one level before getting promoted. Jeff kept referring to this policy, while Scott kept saying that it was unfair and arguing that his great work justified his request. Both men felt frustrated.

A promotion would give Scott a $30,000 yearly increase. What really mattered to him was being able to save $30,000 within a year so he could pay a deposit to buy his first home.

Since Scott kept highlighting the great value he was adding to the team, but never talked about his real need (the salary increase), Jeff thought that he was more interested in the next level's title and the internal company recognition.

Scott was very uncomfortable sharing that he needed more money. He thought the only way for him to increase his compensation was to get a promotion; this is how he had been doing it throughout his career. He grew impatient with the company's promotion policy. Jeff couldn't understand why Scott was questioning this policy, as it was set by the top corporate leaders who are never wrong and who are constantly inspired by the Almighty.

Discouraged by the timeline required for the next promotion and thinking that Jeff was not being supportive, Scott ended up leaving the company. He took a job that gave him a $20,000 salary increase while keeping him at the same level at his new company.

Jeff was surprised by this move. If Scott had been clear on what mattered to him and had communicated that to his boss, Jeff would have been able to get an exceptional approval for a one-shot $30,000 bonus to recognize Scott's work over the past year. Scott would have gotten the money he needed, and he could have waited for the promotion that would come on the usual timeline. He also could have avoided the stress that can come with changing jobs.

DEBRIEF & ADVICE

You have probably realized by now that the start of negotiation from your side is to uncover what REALLY matters to you.

Just as it might not be easy for you to figure out what matters to you, the other party might also find it difficult to determine what they need.

Identifying needs is the responsibility of both parties. And while you must start with your own goals, you can't say "I am clear on my needs; I am done here." You must also help the other side identify their needs and then find ways to meet them in order for the negotiation's outcome to meet your needs. As the saying goes, it takes two to tango.

Jeff is responsible for making the negotiation successful and for keeping Scott on his team. While Scott missed the opportunity to clarify what mattered to him, Jeff could have asked him, "What are you trying to achieve through this promotion? What will this bring to you?"

From your side, you can start by sharing some details about your needs. It's up to you to decide how much you want to share and when you want to share, depending on how the other side is responding. You might not know the other side well, and you might be concerned that they will take advantage of you if you share too much early on. You can say, "I am asking for this because [safe details about your needs]" and gauge the response. Sharing in this way has a double benefit: first, you make the other side aware of at least some of your needs; second, you present a justification for your request. Research shows that justified requests are more likely to be granted than unjustified ones.

Helping the other side uncover their needs is crucial for you and them to reach what matters to both. Scott's needs were clear to him, but he did not know how to articulate them to Jeff, and Jeff did not ask the right questions. You might need to ask several times, in different ways, as the other side's first answers are usually not related to their real needs. To avoid sounding like an interrogator, you can say, "I would like to help you meet your needs so I can meet mine."

When getting stuck in a negotiation, ask yourself, "Are we covering each other's needs here?" Keep in mind this quote, often attributed to J.P. Morgan: "Every person has two reasons for doing anything—a good reason and the real reason."

3 | ARE YOU COMFORTABLE LISTENING? TO OTHERS AND YOURSELF?

STORY

Kevin, a procurement manager, and Christine, a sales representative, recently signed a large construction contract for tens of millions of dollars. The project started 12 months ago and is due to be delivered in four weeks.

Kevin and Christine's companies have been doing business for 10 years. This contract has very bespoke technical specifications. To fulfill her contractual duties, Christine needs to have a subcontractor deliver part of the project.

Christine's subcontractor has just informed her that his delivery will not meet the technical specifications. As per the agreed terms, Kevin is entitled to cancel the contract without any further liability.

Christine's company cannot afford to see this contract

cancelled. They have already spent a lot of cash over the past 12 months, and losing this contract would put the company at risk financially.

Kevin cannot afford to cancel the contract either. No other supplier can deliver this project up to the specifications in four weeks.

The least to say about this situation is that both parties need each other.

Kevin and Christine met three times over the past two days to find a solution. Their last meeting went like this:

Kevin: What else could be done to fix this issue?

Christine: This issue is a top priority. Fixing it…

Kevin interrupting: You keep telling me this is a top priority, but the issue has not been fixed. I care about solutions; I do not care how hard you are trying…

Christine interrupting Kevin back: I also care about finding a solution quickly…

While Christine was talking, Kevin was thinking about counterarguments to Christine's points. They kept arguing and interrupting each other until Kevin told Christine that he was tired of this discussion and considering cancelling the contract. Then he packed his stuff and left the meeting.

DEBRIEF & ADVICE

Christine was about to say that there might be a way to get the subcontractor to meet the specifications, but this additional negotiation was above her pay grade. It would require her CEO to join forces with Kevin's CEO to try to influence the subcontractor's chairman, whom they had both known for a long time.

Christine was unable to present this option, however. When the discussion got heated, she lost her focus on finding a solution. All she was thinking about was how to defend herself, and the more Kevin interrupted her, the more defensive she felt.

It would take Christine and Kevin a few days to calm down, get together, and explore this new option. These few days were precious lost days considering the remaining timeline to deliver the project.

Listening is a key skill that requires practice. When someone is talking and gets interrupted, they continue to play the script in their head and are not really listening to what is being said.

How to be better at listening? Four pieces of advice:

First, don't interrupt. When someone seems to have finished talking, give them a few seconds before jumping in. Maybe they have something else they were just about to tell you, and if you interrupt, you will miss it. Do you need help with waiting? After the person stops talking, say (in your head), "Supercalifragilisticexpialidocious."

This long word should cover the five seconds. Or pick your own word and get used to repeating it in your mind for a few seconds before talking.

Second, get comfortable with silence. This requires practice as well. It is becoming hard to have simple moments of silence during the day. Even when we are alone, we tend to be listening to something. This habit makes our brain constantly crave something to hear. If you observe online meetings nowadays, as soon as someone finishes talking, someone else is jumping in straight away. We are losing the ability to be comfortable with silence, to properly listen to ourselves, to sit down alone with our thoughts. As soon as we have a silent moment with ourselves, our brains are sending signals: "Excuse me, please, can we just change the topic of our discussion? Can you please distract me and distract yourself from me? Thanks in advance."

How to practice silence? Start with 15 minutes to be with yourself with no distraction. I am not preaching any form of meditation here. It could be as simple as going for a walk with no headphones for 15 minutes—just you and yourself and whatever you notice around you.

I accidentally came across the value of silence few years ago. I was coaching a colleague who was sharing a problem he was facing. While he was talking, my head was rushing with several pieces of advice I could give him to magically solve his issue. I was excited about the value I could add. God knows that I love talking a lot, especially when the topic is exciting. My colleague's problem was quite complex. When he finished talking, I was so confused about where to start and how to structure my advice that nothing came from my mouth for a minute. It felt like an eternity. My colleague's face lit up; he then thanked me for giving him the pause to think more about his issue. What? He was thanking me for shutting up. He probably thought I was very good at coaching and was being silent intentionally. He said the momentary silence allowed him not to feel rushed and he felt like there was someone there for him. Guess what I started doing from that day? Shutting up more.

Third, get comfortable with not knowing how to respond when the person stops talking. When you think about your response while they are talking, you are not focusing on the present moment, and you are not listening to them. When discussions are heated, it's tough to refrain from formulating a response, but it's even more important that you focus on listening.

If you are concerned that they might judge you for not responding immediately, you can say, "Look, I would like to focus on what you are saying and hear your view, so I might not be able to give you my perspective straight away. I might need to come back to you later, and take few minutes or hours to think. This does not mean that I agree or disagree with you. It means that I would like to spend my energy focusing on understanding your view instead of on preparing arguments in my mind."

Get used to being comfortable with not knowing and with saying, "I don't know." It probably won't be easy at the beginning. As we grow up, we are expected to know things. At school, we are graded on knowing the answers; then in our jobs, we are expected to know in real time what to do and how to solve problems on the spot. But not knowing something and admitting that can feel liberating.

A final way of staying focused on the present when listening is to take notes. Even if the other person says that you are stupid (this seems unlikely), you can write, "They say I am stupid. Obviously, I don't agree with them." Taking notes forces your mind to stay on the discussion.

4 | HOW DO YOU FEEL? ARE YOU AWARE?

STORY

Suzanne and Gordon used to work together as portfolio managers at an investment and wealth management firm. When the head of portfolio management left, her position became available and both Suzanne and Gordon applied.

The interview and selection period lasted for two months, during which Suzanne and Gordon started getting bitter toward each other. Gordon started finding mistakes in Suzanne's investment advice, sharing them with the head of the office. Suzanne was telling everybody that Gordon was still at a junior level—that he had good potential but still had a lot to learn. (Suzanne had trained Gordon when he joined the firm; she was his mentor.)

Finally, Suzanne was chosen for the role because of her extensive experience and her track record with investments. Suzanne would be Gordon's boss.

Suzanne ultimately found out what Gordon was saying about her work behind her back, and she grew frustrated with him. Gordon felt that the selection process was unfair and did not recognize his potential.

Their interactions became aggressive. They tried to keep the situation to themselves at first but eventually started complaining both to colleagues and to the head of the firm, with Gordon claiming that Suzanne was not treating him fairly, and Suzanne complaining that Gordon was not as effective as he used to be.

Suzanne and Gordon were guided by their frustrations toward each other. They never took the time to openly discuss their issues with each other.

The situation continued for three months, until one day they both got fired.

DEBRIEF & ADVICE

Negotiation is not always about money. I would argue that very often money is just a means to get something deeper, something that really matters. Whenever there is an interaction where two people need to work on something together, it is a negotiation.

For Suzanne and Gordon, their working together was an ongoing negotiation, and it was a failed one because they did not address their emotions.

Emotions are a crucial component of negotiation. If humans are negotiating, their emotions are part of their interactions. This might change one day if other intelligences start negotiating with us or on our behalf, but in the meantime, we still need to deal with our emotions.

All the preparation work you have done and all the strategies you have planned will be useless if you don't consider your emotions. We will focus here on your own feelings and how to handle them.

The moment I feel that my emotions are starting to take control during a negotiation, I ask for a break or ask to regroup at another time or on another day. I say that I am losing focus right now, that I need some time to regroup my thoughts. Most of our counterparts will understand; we are all humans at the end of the day.

To cool down and gain clearer perspectives, you can go for a walk; it is very powerful. As Friedrich Nietzsche wrote in *Twilight of the Idols*, "All truly great thoughts are conceived while walking." I am amazed every time by how my mood shifts between the beginning and the end of a walk.

To refocus your mind, think about what you are trying to achieve from the negotiation and what matters to you. Think as well about what you are losing by letting your emotions drive what you will be doing next. Ask yourself, If I follow the way I am feeling right now, will this help me in meeting my needs? If I stay mad at them and want to hurt them and make them feel bad, will this help me get what I want? Most of the time it won't.

Negative emotions arise usually when we are facing

tough or unusual situations. You have probably heard about getting comfortable with being uncomfortable; I know it might be so cliché, but it's probably one of the best ways to get used to handling your emotions when stakes are high or when situations are unpredictable.

How can this be achieved? By not walking away from facing situations that you expect will make you uncomfortable. The outcome probably won't be good the first few times, but you will get better at handling your emotions as you practice more.

When I took my first job, I thought the salary offer was not high enough. It was the 2007–2008 financial crisis period, and the firm was offering to pay me less than they used to pay people with the same qualifications as mine. When I called the HR person and asked for more, I was uncomfortable; I recall that my whole body was shaking. In my next job negotiations, only my two hands were shaking; then only my left hand was shaking. I usually don't shake now.

Asking someone to play the role of the other side is a good way to practice. Ask someone to play the role of your boss, your customer, your dear partner. See how you react, how you feel. When the real encounter happens, you will be better at handling yourself and anticipating what to expect. Visualizing your emotional state in advance of your encounter with the other side could help in keeping your emotions in check.

Emotions are messages that your body and your

brain are sending you. If you don't listen to these messages, your mental inbox will keep filling up until you get overwhelmed.

Practice listening to your emotions and hearing their messages without letting them control you. Your emotions are not you; what you are feeling does not define who you are. In our fast-paced world, we usually don't have time to listen to our emotions. Either we are at work or spending time with friends or family, and when we are on our own, we watch TV or videos, listen to music or podcasts, or scroll through social media. I might sound like a digital-minimalism advocate, but we have literally no time to sit down (or walk or run) with ourselves and get used to listening to our emotions. It's never too late to take the time to listen to them and be aware of them.

5 | ASK, ASK AGAIN, ASK THE RIGHT PERSON

STORY

While planning a trip for her family, Andrea was able to book the last available room at Maverick Beach resort in Morocco. Because it was school holiday season, there was a very high demand for the hotel.

The trip went as planned until the next-to-last day. That evening, Andrea called the hotel's front desk, asking for a late checkout at 5 pm the next day. (Normal checkout time is 11 am.)

The clerk at the front desk told her that because the hotel was fully booked, they could not offer late checkout. Andrea replied, "Since the next guest's check-in is 3 pm, would you be able to clean my room among the last rooms to be cleaned, and check if some guests are arriving late?" The clerk said the latest they could offer was 2 pm.

Andrea still needed the room beyond 2 pm. Her

youngest daughter was not feeling well and needed to rest before the 9 pm flight home. Andrea knew that staying at the airport for long hours with her two kids would be very tiring.

She asked to speak with the general manager. She first explained that her family loved the experience at the resort, and they were looking to have a final great experience before leaving the country. She then mentioned the flight time and explained that one child was not feeling well. The general manager told her again that the hotel was fully booked and they had no way to extend her room time to 5 pm.

Andrea thought to ask another question: Are all guests expected to check in at 3 pm? She said she was flexible and would be happy to move to another room for a few hours if that would allow them to stay longer.

It turned out that lower-category rooms—cheaper, smaller rooms with no view—are booked for group travelers and one group was due to arrive late in the evening. Andrea was offered two adjacent rooms, and her family could stay until 5 pm. There was no ocean view, but that wasn't a big deal for the last few hours of the trip.

DEBRIEF & ADVICE

Andrea could have just avoided asking for what she needed. The hotel was fully booked, so what was the point of asking, or of asking again? Or of asking a different person? But she asked. What did she have to lose?

If you want to get better at high-stake negotiations, it's best to start practicing on small-stakes negotiations so you can get very comfortable with them and get comfortable with the first step: asking.

We tend to get blocked by ourselves at this first step, but nobody is preventing us from asking.

I have a friend who has been eligible for his next-level promotion for a long time. When I queried him about the reasons he had not been promoted yet, he started explaining all the reasons he was not ready! During the past four years, his department had gone through two changes of management. Each time, he did not ask for a promotion. He believed he still needed more experience, and he thought his two new managers were too new to the role and would not know what it would take to promote him. What he was telling himself was not grounded in reality, however; he was mainly trying to convince himself as he failed to simply ask and begin a discussion.

When he raised the issue with his latest new manager, it turned out that my friend was ready, and he went to his next level in the next promotion cycle.

My friend was concerned that his new managers

would think that he was asking for something he was not ready for. But what would the worst-case scenario be if he asked? There was none, other than being told "no" or "not yet." More likely, asking would have provided a good opportunity for him to get feedback and adjust his strategy for the next time.

Remember Andrea's persistence: She asked the initial question, and she kept asking. When the front desk clerk had clearly reached the limit of what he could offer, Andrea then asked the right person, the decision maker— and she asked a question that led the decision maker to offer a creative solution.

The next time you ask for something and you don't get what you need, don't stop there and think, "Phew, I was brave to ask."

Think, "Did I ask the right person? Did I ask *all* the right persons? Did I ask the right questions?" By doing all of these things, you will probably meet your objectives. You will also increase your confidence in asking more in the future.

We might have been conditioned at school or at work to comply with rules and not think of them as negotiable. If a first authority said no, then we stopped there; we had our internal excuse for not asking again. But if we keep blocking ourselves from the first act of merely asking, we can miss great opportunities. Start by asking; then ask again, ask the right person, and ask other questions. Every time you ask, either you will come closer to getting what matters to you or you will get information to help you with your next move.

The next time you hesitate to ask, think about Andrea's story. Life is too short for not asking, and if you don't ask, you don't get.

6 | WHEN YOU ARE ACTING LIKE A DRAMA QUEEN

STORY

Tino and Pavel are co-owners of an electric car–sharing company in France. For the past few months, they have been looking to expand their business abroad. Through the connections of one their partners, they got in touch with the deputy minister of transport for a country in Africa.

They spent weeks discussing cooperation opportunities with this deputy minister. They were getting very close to aligning on the deal details to roll out Tino and Pavel's service in two cities.

Tino and Pavel felt a good connection with Aissatou, the deputy minister, although they had been talking only through video calls. When both sides felt closer to an agreement, Tino and Pavel decided to fly out to meet Aissatou and the cabinet minister in person. The objective of this meeting was to finalize the last details of the deal and hopefully to sign their cooperation agreement.

On the day of the meeting, Tino felt that Aissatou was more welcoming toward Pavel than toward himself. Tino felt that Aissatou and her team had been mainly addressing Pavel during the discussions.

Feeling that he was being ignored, Tino got annoyed. He was the co-owner of the company and its business mastermind, and he thought his status was being diminished. He started to get difficult through the negotiation, pushing back on items that had been agreed to earlier. He kept mentioning that his company would deliver more value to the ministry of transport than anyone else, hence his request for more money than the amount they had already agreed to.

The whole climate in the meeting became awkward. Where everybody was expecting to close the deal and celebrate, the dynamic moved to Pavel asking to regroup on the next day so he and Tino could discuss the situation and get realigned with each other. The other side accepted that.

It turned out that Aissatou was mainly addressing Pavel because the latter did not speak French properly. He grew up in Poland and had just moved to France one year ago. In wanting to get her messages across correctly to both men, Aissatou had perhaps overdone it by focusing more on Pavel.

DEBRIEF & ADVICE

Tino got emotional. He felt ignored and excluded.

Are his emotions legitimate? Of course they are. How about his reaction? Well, we can argue about that. The main question is, What really matters to him—closing the deal, feeling important, closing the deal *and* feeling important, or something else? This deal was crucial for their company's deployment abroad. It would create a precedent for their first foreign implementation. Tino probably got distracted and acted in contradiction to what matters to him.

What should Tino have done differently? Before letting his emotions drive the show, he could have paused and asked himself, What's going on here? Why would Aissatou act like that? He could have asked for a quick break to talk to Pavel about the situation and get his perspective.

Instead of getting curious, Tino got reactive. It usually feels good to let emotions run the show, but the outcome is usually unpredictable when the emotions are negative. To explain a bad situation to yourself, you create a quick story, and usually this story is negative ("I am being ignored and disrespected!"). Then you shut down your senses and go into drama queen mode, where the situation is about you and the attention you need to have ("How dare they treat me like this?").

Well, you might say this happened only to Tino; it

doesn't happen to me. Let me give you another example close to home. I started a new job, and my self-esteem was quite high, probably overinflated by the counterparts I used to deal with. I arrived late to a meeting. My boss was already talking to the boss of my counterparts, so I started shaking hands with the attendees. When it was time to shake hands with my counterpart's boss, he was so focused on the discussion that he did not shake hands with me; he didn't even look at me. I sat down and was boiling. This affront was an attack on my personality. I, the person chosen by the Almighty and the late Queen of England to negotiate with this company, was ignored by their managing director. Unbelievable.

I will spare you the details of how I acted during the meeting, but you might have guessed. You can bet that the fuss I made was not aligned with what I wanted to achieve with this company or with how I wanted my bosses to see me. Even worse, the situation was not only *not* about me at all; it wasn't even work related. It turned out that the managing director was telling my boss about an emotional incident that happened to his daughter over the summer.

You might say now that this kind of thing happens only to Tino and Anis, never to me, but take some time and think a bit. Our inner dialogue has a high percentage of negative thoughts, so chances are good that if you are exposed to an unclear situation, like Tino and I were, and you don't catch yourself, you are going to have a temporary membership in the drama queen club.

So as a recovered drama queen, my advice, again, is to pause and think, What's going on here? Am I acting in line with what matters to me? You can write these two questions down to get the thoughts from your brain to your notebook or laptop.

Another piece of **advice** is check whether you hang out with people who often act like they are the center of the universe. These people are usually gold and platinum members of the drama queen club.

Why is that? For a couple of reasons:

1. They tend to think that the world is conspiring against them, their perceived fame and status.
2. Whenever you go to them for a perspective on a situation where you acted as a drama queen, they will reinforce your drama queen attitude, like "Who the hell do Johnny or Dasha think they are, acting like that with you?"

Do you recognize these people now?

Let me address the first reason, thinking that the world is conspiring against you. For that to be happening, the world would also be revolving around you. But people are more focused on themselves than they are on you. How many times did you wake up in the morning saying that you are truly excited because you are making Tiffany's life better? (Or worse?) Unless you are the Tiffany you are referring to or she is a loved one to you, the probability is almost zero. You wake up in the morning, brush your teeth or take a shower, and think about yourself and your loved ones.

For the second reason, I bet it's obvious to you now. You are the average of the folks you spend your time with. You are probably asking yourself, "What on earth am I reading here? I bought this book to learn about negotiation and have fun, and this guy is talking to me about who my friends are." Well, my answer is that this book is about getting what matters to you and maximizing your chances of reaching your goals. Make sure your friends don't inadvertently reinforce behaviors that prevent you from getting what matters to you.

7 | THERE IS USUALLY ANOTHER STORY

STORY

Adam has not answered Catherine's emails, calls, or text messages for two weeks now, and his team members haven't responded either.

Though they work for different companies, Catherine and Adam have worked together for five years. Over the past six months, they have been partnering on a bid for a new contract with a joint client. Catherine's main competitor had contacted Adam to work on the same opportunity, but Adam had declined and preferred to work with Catherine's firm. The project appeared to be going smoothly until Adam stopped responding to Catherine's messages.

After not hearing from Adam for two weeks, Catherine was thinking, "For sure, he has already kicked off the partnership with my competitor and they are finalizing their offer to win the deal. He gives no value to our long-term partnership." (During their last call, Adam had been very aggressive, saying that this deal was taking so long to close because of Catherine's company's policies and that he was ready to walk away from the partnership.)

Because Catherine knew Adam's boss quite well, she thought about calling him to complain about the way Adam was putting their long-term partnership at risk. Before making this call, however, she paused for a minute and decided to send a text message to Adam: "Is everything all right?" She got an instant reply: "Let's talk in 5 minutes."

She opened the call by saying, "I do not want to discuss business. I would like to check on how you are. We have known each other for a long time, and I value our relationship more than business opportunities."

Adam informed her that he had been through a lot of trouble within his company because Catherine's firm kept changing the deal's scope. Every time this happened, he needed to go back to various divisions within his firm to ask them to rework the proposal again and again. These repeated requests for changes put his credibility at risk. Nobody was taking him seriously, and his CEO was pressing him to pull out of the deal.

With this information, Catherine realized that Adam was her true advocate and ally within his company. Adam agreed to open the engagement again and to go to their joint client with their final offer.

What a mistake it would have been if Catherine had called his boss!

DEBRIEF & ADVICE

If you constantly believe that your story is the only story and that what you're thinking is among the absolute truths on earth, it will be hard for you to negotiate effectively. All that you will be doing is debating, arguing, or forcing your way when you can.

Why do we jump to conclusions instead of trying to stay curious a bit longer? Our brains like to create shortcuts. There is always a first story that pops up in your mind, and usually this first story is connected to similar situations you have encountered in the past.

You think, "They are stupid, they are evil, they don't get it, they don't like me." Then you start picking up cues from their attitude to confirm your story. And guess what? You start behaving in a way that will probably trigger the other side to behave as you expected. Have you heard about self-fulfilling prophecies?

"They hate me, they are doing this to hurt me, they really want to hurt me." Let me tell you some good news: research shows that no one is really thinking about you all the time. People spend their energy thinking about themselves. Hating someone or planning to hurt someone takes a lot of energy. People spend most of their waking energy thinking about themselves. They seldom think about you, and even more seldom think about hating you.

With that said, I am not telling you that you will never deal with people who will hate you, but probably it will be much less often than you think.

Now that you know that your view of the world is not the only one, let's get you some advice on how to overcome this tendency to jump to conclusions.

When you have a story popping up in your mind about a situation, think of it as an *assumption*—an assumption to be verified, not as an absolute truth.

How can you verify your assumptions? By asking questions to yourself and the other side. In Catherine's case, she did well by calling Adam to find out what was happening before calling the CEO. Her assumption that Adam was the blocker was wrong; if she had followed it, she might have lost any chance to keep the partnership and close the deal.

I am borrowing here a quote from Herb Cohen, one of my heroes on negotiation: "You and I do not see things as they are. We see things as we are."

8 | STAY IN THE PRESENT MOMENT; PICK UP THE CUES

STORY

Martin just moved into a new apartment and went the local branch of SofaTulip to buy a specific sofa he wanted. He felt fortunate that the store had that sofa in stock and could deliver it the next morning. Just one problem: The displayed price of the sofa was $900, but internet retailers were selling it for $650.

When Martin mentioned the price difference to Tony, the store rep, Tony said that the store never matches the prices of online competitors. Martin could buy the sofa for less from one of the internet retailers, but delivery from them would take two weeks and he needed the sofa right away.

Martin used to get discounts at another SofaTulip branch that was near where he lived a few years ago. He mentioned that to Tony, who replied: "I have no leverage on price." Martin got upset and kept arguing with Tony about the discount, saying that Tony's lack of flexibility might push costumers out. Martin left the store and decided not to buy from SofaTulip again.

DEBRIEF & ADVICE

Are you still asking yourself if you are going to be a master negotiator by reading or listening to a story about a sofa? You have probably realized by now that we are negotiating almost all the time. So every opportunity to negotiate is an opportunity to practice and get better. Today you are getting a discount on a sofa; tomorrow you are getting a discount on a house.

Now back to the story: Martin missed the opportunity to stay in the zone and focus on his objective. Staying in the present moment helps you keep your objective in mind (remember, you negotiate to reach your goal, not to demonstrate how clever or awesome you are). More importantly, staying focused helps you pick up cues from your counterpart and react accordingly.

If Martin had stayed focused on his main objective of getting the sofa delivered ASAP, he could have responded differently to Tony's statement ("I have no leverage on price"). He could have asked either or both of the following questions:

- "Is there anyone at the store who has leverage on price?" In this case, Tony's manager had the authority to negotiate, and he could have offered a 20% discount ($180) for new customers.
- "What *do* you have leverage on?" In this case, Tony could have provided free pillows and a small table matching the sofa, free of charge, saving Martin $80. This offer was under Tony's discretion; he usually uses it with nice customers.

Instead, Martin did not stay in the present moment. He time-traveled. Do you wonder how this could be possible?

Here is a quick overview of our brains' time-travel paths:

Option 1: The current situation reminds us of something from the past, and we start dwelling on it. (This is what happened to Martin, as he was accustomed to getting discounts in the past.)

Option 2: We hear a statement from the other side, and we start getting anxious about what this means for the future.

Instead of option 1 or 2, you can choose option 3: you stay in the present.

How you do that? You ask yourself, What's my goal? What's going on? Did I miss anything? Then you ask a question to the other side. Pick any question that comes to mind. This could be as simple as repeating their statement as a question. When Tony said "I have no leverage on the price," Martin could have repeated it but with the intonation of a question: "You have no leverage on price?" This has a double benefit: first, it stops you from time-traveling and forces you to be present. Second, maybe you will learn something new by asking this additional question.

So the next time you are about to board the time machine and travel towards the future or the past, pause, ask a question, and remind yourself to stay a bit longer in the present.

9 | HOW ARE THEY FEELING? HAVE A GUESS

STORY

Paul is meeting Julia today to add his shop to Julia's cupcake franchise. Three years ago, Julia started a franchise agreement with cupcake shops around Amsterdam. Today's meeting is the last one to finalize the details of her deal with Paul's shop.

Paul arrives 15 minutes late, and Julia feels that he is not focused.

Julia: When I listen to you, I feel that something might be bothering you.

Paul: Everything is okay.

Julia: Are you sure?

Paul: I was running late today, so on my way here, I was speeding on the highway, and I got a ticket. And I just got one six months ago.

Julia: Okay. Don't worry; a ticket shouldn't be a big deal. Let's jump to the main topic of our meeting. I am very excited to close this franchise agreement. I am looking forward to a great future together.

Paul: Okay.

Julia: For the revenue sharing, this should be 30/70 for a five-year contract term. Is the duration okay for you or would you consider a longer one?

Paul: I need to think about it.

Julia: What about seven years?

Paul: I am not sure about this anymore. I would like to think about it, so let's meet in a couple of weeks.

DEBRIEF & ADVICE

Julia started the conversation well by mentioning that she is feeling that something might be bothering Paul. However, once he opened up to her, Julia did not acknowledge Paul's emotions or try digging further. Worse, she thought the ticket should be a minor issue. But with Paul getting a second speeding ticket, he's worried that he might be at risk of losing his driver's license. A suspension would affect his business; he really needs his license to deliver cupcakes to his customers, pick up ingredients from his suppliers, and keep his small business running.

Gently telling someone how they might be feeling, if done right, is a powerful tool to diffuse an emotional situation. Why is that and why it is needed in negotiation? Making someone aware of how they feel in a situation can help their rational side take over from their emotional side. You need the rational side of their brain to be in control so you can have a constructive discussion and negotiation with them. The emotional side of their brain (the limbic system) could make them take a decision that goes against even their own self-interest. I won't be delving into the neuroscience behind this; you can do an online search for "limbic system and amygdala hijack." My aim here is to show you how to help people become aware of their feelings.

(Don't tell them how you think they *should* be feeling, or not feeling. You are making a non-judgmental guess about how they are feeling; that's it. You are not lecturing them on what emotions they should or should not have.)

Your attempt to identify their emotion sends the message that you care about them. Even if your guess is wrong, you are showing that you are making an effort to understand how the person feels. By signaling your willingness to fully listen, you give them an opportunity to talk more and to say, "Well, actually, I feel [nervous/scared/worried/sad/whatever]."

A suggestion on how to make this guess is to say, "In

listening to you, I hear [this emotion] in your voice." Their brain will be saying, "Wow, this is someone who is taking the time to try to understand how I feel. Also, hang on—yes, it seems that I feel angry here." Or "Your guess is incorrect; this is how I feel."

Keep the focus on them. It's not about you; it's about them here. How many times have we shared our tough situation with someone, only to have them say that they fully understand it—and then start telling you a story about a similar situation that happened to them? Every experience is unique (at least for the person living it). The person telling you their own story might think of their approach as a good way to connect with you, but it might have the opposite effect. After all, they are not you, they have not lived your life, you don't have the same background, and you probably don't have the exact same vision for your future.

Remember, when you are the one who is listening to someone and trying to hear their emotion, you need to be genuinely interested in that person. If you are feigning interest for the sake of showing that you are the most empathic person in town, the other side will probably feel the lack of sincerity. Instead of connection, there will be distance and perhaps less trust. That outcome will help neither your relationship with the person nor the goal you want to reach through your negotiation.

10 | IF THEY LIKE YOU

STORY

George lives five hours away from London but owns a flat there. He has rented it to Andrew for almost a year, and the tenancy contract is about to expire.

When there were some plumbing issues at the beginning of the tenancy, Andrew was very aggressive in dealing with George, who did his best to fix the problems quickly. Following this incident, George agreed to do some renovation work that Andrew requested.

To partially cover the renovation costs, George decided to raise the rent for the new tenancy period. Andrew and George were due to have a call about that.

George expected a heated discussion with Andrew; after all, nobody wants to have their rent raised. However, George was pleasantly surprised that Andrew started their call by asking questions about him. Andrew wanted to get to know him better, and said that he regretted not having had the opportunity to do so before.

George was a farmer. Andrew said that during his childhood, his father took him to visit his friends' farms on most weekends and he loved that. George told him about his farming activities and the challenges he was facing during this harvest period. Andrew showed great interest in George's experience.

Andrew shared that he and his spouse just had their first baby, and he talked about how life-changing this was, with both the joy and the required work. George has two grownup kids.

When they finally talked about the tenancy contract, Andrew said that he would like to stay for another year, but he needed the rent to remain the same. He reminded George that he had managed the workers during the renovation period, saving George the hassle of driving five hours to London and doing that himself. Also, Andrew requested some extra work to be done during the new tenancy period. Finally, Andrew said that he realized that he might have come across as aggressive, but when the plumbing issues happened, his baby was due shortly and he urgently needed the problems to be fixed. He apologized for his attitude.

George agreed to keep the rent as it was, and he agreed to do the extra work—not immediately, but within the next four months, as he was facing a cash flow shortage.

DEBRIEF & ADVICE

During their conversation, George came to like Andrew, understanding that he was not as aggressive as George had initially believed. He thought, "Here is a person trying to take care of his kids, like me."

Also, George realized how valuable it was to have Andrew save him the hassle of coming from his town to manage the workers in London every time renovations were underway.

Furthermore, George decided that he preferred to deal with Andrew, whom he already knew and liked, rather than take chances with a new unknown tenant.

People tend to like to deal and make deals with people they like. We enjoy being around people who make us feel good about ourselves.

The first thing needed for the liking to happen is to be warm and interested in the other person. Ask questions and listen to the person's stories. Everyone has a story to tell; you need to dig for it. Usually, common interests or common challenges help us bond with the other party. For George and Andrew, these interests and challenges were spending time on farms and raising children.

If you have some negative history with the other side, try to clarify it before going further. We are all humans (at least for now before AI gets more in the game). People generally do understand that we might go through tough times and make wrong calls. If you leave negative history unspoken, it will fuel negative stories in the other person's mind, making them less eager to help you.

The next time you are negotiating, in addition to discussing the deal's details and all the preparations you have done, leave some room to pause and inquire about the other person's story and life experience. They will probably like and value that interest.

11 | HOW ABOUT WE LOOK AT IT FROM ANOTHER ANGLE?

STORY

Elif is a manager at one of the branches of the LePainduFour restaurant chain. She started as a waitress and worked her way up to the management position over the past three years.

With her recent promotion, Elif got a salary raise, but she felt that it was not enough. Because of a staff shortage among waiters, she was working extra shifts to wait tables in addition to working her management shifts. This situation went on for more than 12 months.

She talked with Mika, her manager, about what needed to be done to increase her salary. Mika asked Deepak, the general manager of the chain. Deepak was surprised by Elif's request for higher pay, as he believed they were paying her top-of-the-market salary. Having worked at other restaurant chains, Deepak was very aware of salary levels in their market. He thought Elif's request was unrealistic, and he was convinced that even if Elif decided to go elsewhere, she wouldn't get more.

The whole discussion went nowhere. Mika told Elif that she should be grateful for the opportunity they were giving her and that her compensation would increase over the coming years while she grew more in her role, but nothing would be done now or in the near future.

Do you think that Elif left it there? Let's see.

She brought up the topic again with Mika, sharing her frustration of being overworked without getting any reward for it. This discussion also went nowhere and created some tension between them.

One day, however, Elif thought about looking at the situation from Mika and Deepak's perspective. She thought, "They are right. I won't get more if I go elsewhere; I can't deny it. But if I decide to go elsewhere, what would be the real cost for them to bring in a new manager, whom the team trusts, who knows all the logistics in and out, and who can be independent from day one?" The staffing shortage and high turnover among the team were caused by the previous manager, whom Elif replaced.

She went back to Mika again, this time with a different approach.

Elif: Hey, Mika, I thought about our previous discussions. You and Deepak are right. I won't get more elsewhere, and the salary here is good compared to the competition.

You know, Mika, I am very grateful for the opportunity. I know you have been vouching for me.

The thing is, managing the team while filling in for the staff shortage is requiring more commitment and extra shifts. It is making me spend less time with my family and giving me less time to pursue other activities I have in mind.

With the compensation I am getting and this level of commitment, I am wondering if this is the best investment opportunity for myself. Would there be another investment where I could get a better return in the mid and long term—maybe not necessarily in our industry? Going back to university and transitioning my career to marketing could be one option. So the options I am thinking of are not really limited to just going to another restaurant chain.

I know that Deepak and you were thinking that I can't get my current salary in another restaurant, and rightly so. Now I would like to suggest another perspective: How about not thinking about how much I could get by going to competitors, but thinking about the real cost for LePainduFour if I decided to go and do something else with my life?

What would the consequences be if you hired a new manager? When the manager role was open and I applied, you interviewed several applicants and you realized how hard it is to get the right fit. Also, how long would the new manager need to ramp up, to establish themselves with the team, and to have a good impact on reducing turnover? What would be the impact of that transition on the restaurant's productivity, on the quality of our service?

Mika: Let me speak to Deepak again.

Mika came back and offered a one-time bonus to Elif. They were not able to review her current salary, but Deepak had some budget left from last year's training expenses that he was able to use for the one-off payment.

DEBRIEF & ADVICE

Both sides had their views on the situation, and both sides thought their views were valid. Hey, who would say, "I have an opinion, I believe it strongly, and by the way this opinion is rubbish"?

Both sides were looking at the other side as delusional. "Why are they behaving like that? For sure it is personal; they don't like me." How many times have you looked at a situation and concluded "they don't like me"?

Elif's first two negotiation attempts failed. Then she

did something that is the basis of any successful negotiation: she asked herself first how the other side was looking at the situation.

Elif told Mika that her and Deepak's view was valid. (Negotiations often fail at the beginning as the parties start by arguing about the other's side is not valid.) Then she offered to view the situation from another perspective and think about consequences down the line.

A way to do that is to say, "I agree with your view" (the other side will feel relieved). Then say, "I would like to offer another perspective." Explain this new angle, and then ask, "Have you thought about the consequences if we all go down the path of this new view?"

When Mika and Deepak thought about the situation from the new perspective, they realized two things. First, Elif had more options than they thought; she was not limited to going to a competitor's chain. She could even go start collecting mushrooms and vlogging about it as a full-time job. Second, if she left, they would be in trouble that would cost them more than a salary increase or a one-time bonus.

Using this technique is like holding a picture frame and telling the other side, "I respect your frame. How about you look at this picture through the frame I am holding and think about consequences, and then make up your mind?"

12 |IF WE CAN DO IT AGAIN?

STORY

Alfonso is the Middle East sales director at a global internet service provider with headquarters in Spain. Sami is the head of the internet service department at the ministry of technology in one of the Middle Eastern countries. His department oversees the selection of a few reliable global service providers to provide internet services to serve the country. For the past two years, Alfonso has tried, without success, to get a meeting with Sami.

Alfonso recently hired Ali as an account manager. Ali tried to initiate contact with Sami by connecting with people from his team. Ali heard that Sami was recently struggling as one of his key suppliers caused several outages that impacted the internet in a large part of the country.

Through Sami's team, Ali was able to finally get Sami's attention. Sami emailed both Alfonso and Ali, offering to explore working together if they would offer their service on a free trial period of six months. This was feasible to them as they had plenty of internet capacity available.

Without consulting with Ali, Alfonso sent a long email back to Sami, telling him about his company's great services. He mentioned that a six-month trial was not in line with industry standards, but he would agree to a one-month trial maximum.

Surprised by Alfonso's email, Sami replied that the six-month trial was needed to test the service's reliability and to feel comfortable using them permanently as a key supplier for the country.

Alfonso replied straight away that he is a major supplier to most of Sami's neighboring countries, and he could provide reference letters from their ministries of technology, but the best and final trial period he could agree to was two months.

Radio silence from Sami.

Alfonso and Ali tried to chase Sami, offering to have a call to resume their discussion, but received no reply for a month. Alfonso thought the deal was a lost cause.

Ali, however, had an upcoming trip to the Middle East. He sent a message to Sami, telling him that he would be visiting his country and would like an opportunity to meet. Sami replied, offering to meet at his office.

At the meeting:

Ali: We are really eager to work with you, and we are confident we will provide a great service to the users in your country. It seems there was a misunderstanding in our recent communication, so I would like to ask: If we could start over, what would you advise?

Sami: The six-month trial period is a deal-breaker. Over the past several years, the process of selecting suppliers has gotten stricter, as many partners stopped providing their services at the highest standards they initially promised. Six months is the minimum for our engineers to see sustained stability and reliability. I understand that you are providing internet services to neighboring countries, but we need to test the service for ourselves and be fully convinced. As you have enough internet capacity to serve the Middle East, providing the service free of charge should be a no-brainer for you. We can discuss, though, the limit of capacity to be provided free of charge for the trial period. We are not trying to take advantage of this situation; you understand that several global internet providers are very eager to work with us, and we need to make sure to select the best ones. The door is open if you can meet this condition.

Ali: Thanks a lot for your feedback. Let me discuss this with my management and I will get back to you quickly.

After getting management approval, Ali confirmed the feasibility of the trial with Sami. The six-month period went very well, and Ali's company became among the three top internet service providers in the country in less than a year.

DEBRIEF & ADVICE

Alfonso and Sami got into a deadlock situation. Alfonso's position was that two months was the maximum trial period, while Sami had six months as a deal-breaker. They did not make an effort to understand each other's motivation, and communication got cut short. When a deal falls apart, it's easy to think that this is the other side's responsibility, not yours, and that they don't get it or they are too greedy or whatever evil thing you could think of them. This is how Alfonso and Sami might have felt about each other.

Ali helped unlock this situation by asking one single question:

"If we could start over, what would you advise us to do?"

This question helped Sami to open up more about his intentions and constraints.

Imagine that both parties have walked away from the deal or are about to walk away from it. If you then come and ask this question, you will be sending several signals:

1. You are open to looking at the situation from a different perspective.
2. You value the other person. People feel valued when asked for advice.
3. You simply show respect for the other side.
4. You might be giving them a way to come back to the negotiation. They might have cornered themselves into a position and gotten stubborn about it; by asking this question, you allow them to create new openings.

You might think that asking this question will show a weakness or a neediness from your side. You are not committing to anything, though; you have already demonstrated that you have walked or are ready to walk away. What you are really showing is more curiosity about the other side. The question starts with "If," and you can still walk away from the negotiation if you don't like what they say or offer.

If you are still concerned about showing weakness by asking for advice, you can start by calling out the fact that you have walked away already. Say something like, "Now that we have demonstrated to each other our ability to walk away, what would you advise to get us on track to find a deal that generates more value for both of us?"

13 | WHAT ARE THEY TELLING THE WORLD?

STORY 1

Anna lives in London. This winter season has been cold, and her heating has been down for more than a day, so she called her gas supplier to get it fixed.

"The earliest we can do is within three days," said the representative on the phone.

Anna said that she has a one-year-old baby and has no way to keep the whole house warm for three days. She explained that portable heaters are not good for her son.

"We are not an emergency company, madam. To get an express service within the same day, this will cost you 350 pounds plus VAT. For that fee, you can get a technician in 24 hours," said the rep.

Anna checked the company's website and found its mission statement: "Feeling great for taking the right decisions."

Anna replied, "I checked your company website, and it mentions that your core value is 'Feeling great for taking the right decisions.' Do you feel great for taking the right decision for me and my baby?"

The line went silent for 30 seconds. Then the rep replied that he will send a technician to her home in the afternoon, free of charge.

STORY 2

Laila's glasses were broken by her baby daughter. Laila urgently needed to get them repaired, as her eyesight was so bad that she could hardly see without her glasses. Fortunately, she had contact lenses at home. However, she couldn't use them for more than a couple of days as they made her eyes dry.

That same day, Laila went to the nearest optician, a company that her husband had used recently. They were advertising that they were proud to be a family business running for more than 80 years within their community. Nikesh, the manager, seemed helpful. He understood Laila's situation and promised to have the glasses repaired in 24 hours.

When Laila returned with her husband the following day, Nikesh said the glasses were not ready yet and advised the couple to call in the afternoon. When the couple called, Nikesh told them the glasses were in the lab, and he would have them ready tomorrow morning.

Laila and her husband went back in the morning, and they got into a heated discussion with Nikesh. He had no glasses and no updates. Laila asked for a refund. She was frustrated, as she had already lost two days and she would need to wait even longer if she went to another optician. Nikesh refused. He had already paid the lab for the repair, and he said he couldn't do anything more.

Laila went back home and called Nikesh. She first apologized for the heated discussion. She then told Nikesh that the main reason she came to him was that her family always prefers to shop at local stores to support the businesses within the community. She mentioned that Nikesh's business was a family one that was probably started by his grandparents and that helping the community seems to be important to them. Then she asked, "Do you feel that your family business supported me as part of the community in this situation?"

Laila got her glasses that afternoon. Nikesh drove an hour and half to the lab, staying there with the technician until the glasses were repaired, and then he brought them back to his shop.

DEBRIEF & ADVICE

People often do their best to stay consistent with their values, or what they claim their values are, and companies do the same. These values are like promises they are making to the outside world. When you are dealing with someone and they are acting in a way that does not align with what they are claiming as their values, go ahead and call it out. But call it out in a way that leaves it to *them* to come to the conclusion that their behavior is inconsistent with what they have promised.

So instead of telling Nikesh that the late repair and broken promise went against what his family business stands for, Laila asked a question to help him think about his company's values. And instead of telling the gas company that they were not making the right decision, Anna asked a question and let the other side come to their own conclusion.

People often do their best to stay consistent—but they don't like to be cornered. When you make a statement, you corner them, and most people will get defensive, fight back, and keep arguing.

If you are negotiating with a company, ask them, "Is what you are doing right now in line with your core values?" If you are dealing with a person who has claimed to be transparent (but hasn't been), ask, "Is the way you are acting right now in line with what you told me earlier about transparency being an important value to you?"

14 | RUSHING, RUSHING

STORY

Khalil and Natalia bought their first home in London. They were moving in three weeks, so they needed to buy a dining table and a bed.

They went to their usual furniture store. After they browsed for a while, Giuseppe, one of the floor sales reps, approached them, offering to help. They explained that they were looking for a king-size bed and mattress and that delivery speed was crucial for them.

Giuseppe started showing them the models in stock. The couple seemed to like one of them, but it was beyond their budget.

> Giuseppe: This is our bestseller. We have been making this model for the past five years.
>
> The couple: Hmmm…

Giuseppe: My in-laws just bought the same model; they are super happy with it.

The couple: Great.

Giuseppe: What do you think?

The couple: We like it. It seems comfy.

Giuseppe: We have some bedsheets that would match—all organic products. We can deliver them at the same time; let me show you.

The couple: They look nice.

Giuseppe: Would you need an assembly service? With Covid, our team takes all required safety measures.

The couple: Probably, yes.

Giuseppe: While you are choosing the bedsheet color, let me start putting your order into the system.

Giuseppe: Already reserved the bed for you. Let's go to see the dining table. How do you prefer to pay?

The couple: We are not sure; we need to think about it.

Giuseppe, annoyed: But you told me that you need these quickly. If you come back tomorrow. I'm not sure if they will still be there.

The couple: Thanks a lot. Have a nice day.

Giuseppe was surprised. He did everything by the book, he was enthusiastic, he was asking questions, but still the couple left without buying.

DEBRIEF & ADVICE

Giuseppe is your usual sales rep—very nice, very chatty—but his demeanor was too hyper for Khalil and Natalie. The couple needed some breathing space to think and decide. Giuseppe was so eager to sell that his brisk pace felt like pressure to the couple.

Because the couple told Giuseppe that they needed the furniture quickly, he assumed that they would jump on the first model they liked. He did not know that the model was beyond the couple's budget or that they were not the kind of buyers who decide on the spot. He started rushing them into deciding, instead of allowing them to follow their own pace.

Giuseppe wanted this deal done. It was nearly the end of the month, and he was short on his sales target. He was so focused on his objectives that he missed the fact that it takes two parties to make a deal.

What could Giuseppe have done differently after showing the couple the models? Either of two things:

- Giuseppe could have given Khalil and Natalia some space, telling them that he would be around if they needed more help. The couple would have been able to talk to each other privately, think about the decision, and maybe decide to go over their available budget by paying in monthly installments.
- Giuseppe could have simply stayed with them and remained silent.

We saw two key factors of a decision-making process in play: time and autonomy. Giuseppe failed to appreciate both.

First, time: He assumed that his perception of the pace of time was the same as the couple's. He was in a hurry to close the sale, and the couple told him they needed an early delivery, so he thought this was his lucky day.

You need to understand and adjust to the other side's pace and perception of time. Time is relative. The way we perceive it in a negotiation might be different from the way our counterparts perceive it, depending on our motivations or our constraints.

One way to understand the perception of time is to ask and verify. For the "ask" part, Giuseppe could have just said to the couple, "I understand you are looking for a quick delivery. We looked at several models. Are you wanting to make a purchase today or do you feel you need more time to browse?" Most of the time, the other side will give you an idea about their timeline, about their perception of time. Some won't, for whatever reasons. Some people might worry that you would take advantage of their hurry and pressure them; others might plan to use time to take advantage of you.

This is where the "verify" part comes into play. You can observe whether what they are telling you about their timelines aligns with how they are acting. For example, in the corporate world, a buyer might push their suppliers to provide their best and final offers early in the negotiation because the buyer needs to make a decision and sign the contract quickly. However, once asked by their suppliers for more details about the decision process or timelines or for extra meetings to determine the best solutions for the buyer's requirements, the buyer might start to be vague and unavailable. Perhaps they don't provide all of the necessary information or they don't answer messages or return phone calls. If the other side is saying that they are in hurry on a matter but the way they are behaving does not show that, this is an example of misalignment and it should raise a question mark on your side.

Now for the second component: autonomy. Giuseppe was pushing to close the order, and the pressure probably overwhelmed Khalil and Natalie. They probably felt obliged to place an order, but they were not yet convinced about the purchase. When you force someone to decide, you limit their autonomy. Autonomy is one of our core emotional drivers. You are more motivated and fulfilled when you perceive that you have free will and control of your decisions. You will feel the opposite if your autonomy is threatened. How do you feel when you are forced into something or someone else is deciding for you?

How can you avoid limiting the other side's autonomy? By making it clear that it is their decision.

Giuseppe could have said, "Sometimes it can feel like there's too much to choose from, and you might need to think through all the options. Just to let you know, these beds go very quickly, as they have the shortest delivery timelines. If you are interested in getting this bed, I advise that you place an order today. I am not trying to pressure you, though; it's your choice. I will be around helping other customers, so give me a shout if you need me."

15 | WHO IS INFLUENCING THEM?

STORY

Sam is the owner of a startup that makes organic juices for kids. Having only limited success with selling online, he was trying to get into one of the largest organic food stores in Berlin. He had several meetings with the owner, Frank, to persuade him to display his top product, HanzGrettel, on his store's shelves.

Frank's store had built a strong brand around organic foods, and a lot of celebrities with millions of followers bought their organic groceries from this store. If Frank agreed to cooperate with Sam, it would be a great advertisement for HanzGrettel.

Frank's office was on the top floor of the store. The small office next to it belonged to Tobias.

Before their meetings, Sam used to sit in the lounge outside of Frank's office, waiting. He would wave hello to Tobias, but he never engaged in a discussion. On several occasions, Tobias came out to have a chat with Sam and enquired about his business, but Sam was cold and brushed him off. Sam has never bothered to understand what Tobias was doing at Frank's company. Sam was thinking that Tobias might be an accountant or one of Frank's administrative assistants, and he did not want to spend time or energy with him. He thought he needed to keep his focus on Frank.

There was no progress, meeting after meeting. Sam got frustrated until one day Frank told him clearly that he was not interested in displaying his product.

It turned out that Tobias was Frank's close friend. Tobias had been there for Frank ever since he opened the store 20 years ago. Meanwhile, Sam was thinking that Frank was just a stupid guy who did not realize what he was missing out on.

DEBRIEF & ADVICE

Frank and Tobias spoke about Sam and his company at one of their catch-ups. Tobias was concerned about Sam as a future partner. Frank's store was a family business, with respect and fairness at the heart of it. Frank had zero tolerance for jerks, even if they were superstars. From his discussion with Tobias, he made up his mind about Sam.

What did Sam fail to do? First, he forgot to be kind and respectful. Second, he missed the opportunity to understand who could influence Frank on his decision. If he had done a bit of research, he could have understood the men's friendship. How could he have figured this out? By talking to the staff at the supermarket, checking Frank's company registry (where Tobias is listed as a shareholder), and being more curious when Tobias came over to chat with him.

Let's go back to being kind and respectful. What would it have cost Sam to take a few minutes to chat with Tobias and answer his questions? Probably nothing. These conversations would have occurred while Sam was already sitting in the lounge, waiting for Frank. Being respectful does not cost much, and it has a massive upside. There is this popular saying: when you are going to your flat on the top floor, don't forget to say hello to your neighbors on the ground floor, as you are going to meet them again on your way down.

You have probably seen by now that a negotiation starts well *before* you engage with the other side, with the decision maker. The latter rarely operate on their own; they typically have people who help with advice. Some of them are clearly identified and others are hidden; you need to identify both to increase your chances to influence them, to get what matters to you.

Just look at kids to see how they do it. If Mummy is the decision maker for more TV, I will go to Daddy, if not to the grandparents, looking for someone to influence her.

I will leave you here with a personal story. When I started as a junior account manager, I was trying to develop a business relationship with one of the companies in the Middle East. My issue was that I was unable to get a call with the general manager, the one who says the final yes. The company I worked for had no business history with this customer. Did I leave it there? I think by now you can guess the answer.

I found a younger buyer (probably the most junior buyer they had) who was ready to pick up my calls. To build rapport, I started sharing with him views about the industry. Soon enough, he looped in his manager. Three months down the line and still no business. Then they started giving me small orders. Then I started getting medium-size orders. Then one day, a bid opportunity of around $5.5 million came in.

I was thinking I had almost zero chance of winning this bid. My competitor's CEO was meeting the general manager, regularly going to lunches and dinners with him. But I persisted and worked through the opportunity. I will spare you the deal details, but a few weeks after submitting my proposal, I got a phone call from the junior buyer, asking me to prepare the contract to sign the deal. At that stage, I had never met the general manager or spoken to him. I had never met the junior buyer or his manager in person; I had only talked to them on the phone. We had not even seen each other's faces; there was no Zoom or Microsoft Teams or WhatsApp at that time.

When we finally met in person a couple of months later, I learned that the general manager's organization was vouching for me and the high quality of service and support I had provided to them on the small and medium projects. I understood that the junior buyer and his manager had significant influence on the selection of suppliers. My competitors were in touch mainly with the general manager and had very little engagement with the junior buyer and his manager—the people whose opinions carried the most weight.

It pays to develop relationships with the decision makers and with people who influence them.

16 | ARE YOU THE ULTIMATE BOSS?

STORY

Tim brought his car to LocallyGarage to have new tires put on. Theresa quoted 1200£ + VAT with a fitting in three days. Tim offered to pay 590£ + VAT, saying that he paid this price a couple of years ago for similar tires.

Theresa replied that the garage does not stock tires for Tim's car brand, so they needed to be ordered specially for him. Regarding his discount request, she would need to talk to her business partner and phone Tim back in the afternoon.

Theresa phoned Tim few hours later and told him that the best price they would agree to was 1080£ + VAT and that she would try to get the tires within one business day. Tim was happy with the offer; he placed the order straight away.

Chapter 16

DEBRIEF & ADVICE

Theresa did not want to react immediately to Tim's request and needed to think about it. She knew that matching his price request would not be feasible. The best she could do was 980£ + VAT. She needed to think about what else she could do beside the price; in this case it was a quicker delivery.

Also, she and her business partner have a rule not to react immediately to nonstandard requests from customers. Instead, they allow themselves a few hours before deciding, preferably checking with each other during that time. They made this rule for themselves because agreeing to customers' discount requests on the spot had caused problems. Theresa and her business partner realized that they were not aligned with each other on the prices they were offering, and the misalignment created a mess for accounting and for customer relationships. Following their rule to wait, think, and check with each other meant they gave consistent answers.

Even if you are a boss—by boss, I mean the true decision maker for the negotiation in hand—you can always consult with and refer to another authority who might have a say in the matter. This authority could be a spouse, a business partner, or a decision committee. In the corporate world, the common setup is to have a negotiation team that leads the negotiation within the defined scope of a mandate. The decision maker doesn't usually step into the negotiation. The objective of this setup is to provide the negotiation team with a fallback to consult with for any further decisions and not to be pressured to make calls on the spot.

Once the decision maker/boss steps into the negotiation, the other side might expect that they are now dealing with someone with the highest power, who can give them what they want and who can decide on the spot. Also, decision makers probably have bigger egos and tend to show it. The other side might take advantage of that, challenging their egos and pushing them to agree to larger concessions that were not planned.

The aim of this story is to suggest that you build the habit of consulting with and referring to another party. Most decisions can wait for a bit of time before being made. Referring to another party that you need to consult with gives you the bandwidth to think through the issue and gain other perspectives before making a commitment.

17 | LET THEM BE THE BOSS, IF THEY WANT TO

STORY

Chris, senior buyer at CoffeeTop, a coffeehouse chain, and Mike, head of sales at Orgabrew, a coffee supplier, held a meeting because CoffeeTop shortlisted Orgabrew as a potential supplier for a new line of coffee. The final decision was to be made within a month.

Mike happens to know Rudy, the CEO of CoffeeTop. They went to university together 20 years ago and are part of the same neighborhood community.

At the beginning of the meeting, Mike asked Chris if Rudy would be attending the meeting, although the meeting attendees were known in advance and Rudy was not expected to attend.

During the discussions, Mike asked Chris what Rudy thought about a specific point. Chris seemed annoyed, replying that he was the one in charge of the selection process and that Rudy was not directly involved.

At the end of the meeting, Mike told Chris that when he saw Rudy at a community lunch on Saturday, he would give him a summary of their discussions.

A few weeks later, Mike was informed that CoffeeTop selected another supplier.

DEBRIEF & ADVICE

Mike kept showing Chris that he had access to his CEO, and the repeated mentions seemed to undermine Chris's authority. It turned out that the procurement process at CoffeeTop was not under the CEO's control, and Chris had the full power to choose the new supplier.

What could Mike have done differently? He could have briefly mentioned his connection to the CEO at the beginning of the meeting and left it there. He then could have asked Chris for advice to acknowledge his authority: "As a senior buyer at CoffeeTop and the decision maker in this process, what advice would you give to Orgabrew to be in a position to support you on your new product line?"

Chris was the decision maker and had a certain level of authority in this situation, but Mike failed to acknowledge that. He kept challenging it despite all the signals from Chris that he was the one in charge.

When engaging in a negotiation, try to figure out

how the other side perceives their status and authority within the negotiation. Sometimes this is straightforward: they are the head of the department; they are sitting in the boss's chair at the head of the table; they are probably sending signals about their high status in this environment. In other situations, you will need to figure this out during the early encounters with them by trying to understand what they are proud of. How? By asking them more questions about themselves. What are they excited about? Where do they feel fulfilled? What achievements are they proud of within the context at hand? The answers will help you identify their perceived status, as people usually don't hide status or authority honor badges.

Their perceived status is situational and is not absolute to all aspects of life (even Queen Elizabeth's and President George Washington's statuses were situational). Someone's status as a team manager is limited to the environment within their team. They would not have the same authority within other teams, or when they go to the supermarket or when they go to yoga class with their friends.

Once you figure out their perceived status in the situation, my advice to you is to acknowledge it and avoid challenging it. When you challenge their status or decide to ignore it, you will be stepping into Ego Land, the land where emotional egos control every decision and thought. They People will then get emotional and will start to display their authority by retaliating. This challenge and response will shift the focus from achieving each other's goals to displaying power.

In the corporate world, I frequently hear people name-dropping executives on a project to show a connection with them or to imply that these executives have already given their approval, signaling that whatever discussion the other side might be having with you is just a formality. If you were on the receiving end of this name-dropping, how would it make you feel?

At home, couples might compete to show who is the boss in a given situation, instead of focusing on the issues to be solved for kids, holidays, or anything else. There is probably no absolute boss in a couple. One partner might be the boss when it comes to the kids' academic education, but not their sports education; the other partner might be the boss when it comes to organizing holidays. Fighting about who is the absolute boss would just be a distraction.

Acknowledging the other side's status could start as simply as asking them how they see the situation: "Considering your background and experience in this situation, I would love to hear your perspective."

Remember, a negotiation is not a competition to see who has the highest status, who is smarter, or who has the larger fan base. Your aim is to keep both sides focused on getting what matters.

18 | A ONE-OFF MOVE

STORY

Adam, a junior account manager at a media agency, was contacted by John, a senior procurement manager at a large pharmaceutical firm. John requested Adam's best offer on a new campaign his firm was launching. Although the companies had not done business with each other before, John stated that the offer should be provided within 48 hours, and that a decision would be made within 10 days.

In Adam's industry, developing similar proposals typically takes several weeks. Adam wanted to land this new customer, though, so he heavily mobilized several team resources and was able to provide the proposal on time, on a Friday at 11 pm.

On Sunday morning, John called Adam, asking for a 25% price reduction to seal the deal. He expected an answer no later than Monday morning. This was a significant reduction, but Adam was very eager to get this deal, as it would help him make his yearly sales target and land a new customer at the same time. He needed the approval from his boss, who had just left for vacation, and from his marketing vice president, who was out of town on a family weekend. He reached out to both. After some discussions, they agreed to offer the price reduction, with Adam guaranteeing to the vice president that the deal would be done. Adam called John straight after to let him know that his company had agreed to the price reduction.

At noon on Monday, Adam called John, expecting to hear good news and to send him the contract to be signed. No reply. He tried several times during the day without success. John finally answered late in the evening, and said that they had to go with Adam's competitor for strategic reasons!

When Adam met John one month later at a trade-show, Adam explained that what happened put him in a bad spot with his management. He also suspected that John had used him to lower the competition's offer—a suspicion that turned out to be accurate. John jokingly told him that what happened was an accepted negotiation behavior in the industry and that Adam should have seen it coming. It turned out that John was lying to Adam about his intentions. He never intended to award the business to Adam; he was using Adam's offer to pressure his existing supplier to lower their price.

Ten years later, Adam becomes head of sales at his agency, a leader in their industry now. John is the head of marketing and procurement in his organization. John's company is launching a new product, for which Adam's agency would be the perfect partner.

Adam has a good memory...

DEBRIEF & ADVICE

You might have heard about or experienced similar situations. You might have already been advised not to be deceptive.

Deceptive behaviors might be unplanned for the deceiving side. People might find themselves under pressure, and before they realize what they're doing or think about the consequences, they lie to their counterparts. Then they build up on the lie and before they realize it, they become deceptive as a matter of habit.

Some advice to prevent that from happening: First, prepare your negotiation in advance. Second, if you find yourself in a stressful negotiation, take time out to think about your next move. Finally, if you do lie, then apologize, say that you provided confusing information, and provide the truth.

If you are among the people who plan to be deceptive, just remember that people have good memories and there is always a tomorrow.

On the other side, if you are in a situation similar to Adam's, you can start by checking your counterpart's background. After being deceptive for some time, your counterpart might have gained a reputation for dishonesty, so check with your peers.

You can also document your discussions. After every discussion, Adam could have sent a quick memo to John, looping in bosses from both sides and asking for John's confirmation of his correct understanding of their discussions. A deceptive person tends to avoid leaving proof of their actions.

Finally, try to involve more people in the process. Adam could have organized a quick call involving John and both of their bosses and including the technical and marketing teams from both sides. The more the merrier. A deceptive person tends to back off when a large group is involved.

PART II
GETTING WHAT MATTERS—WITH KIDS

19 | PARENTS, KEEP NURTURING YOUR KIDS' ABILITIES

STORY

I told my five-year-old daughter that she negotiated well in one situation. When she asked me what negotiation means, I tried to explain, and it went like this:

Me: What do you do when you ask Daddy for an ice cream and Daddy says no?

Her: I wait for Daddy to be super-duper happy and I ask him again.

Me: What if Daddy still says no?

Her: Maybe he says no for now. I ask him then if I can get it later today.

Me: What if he says no again?

Her: I ask him why.

Me: What if he keeps saying no?

Her: I go and ask Mummy.

Her answers made me smile. She said, "Daddy, you are super-duper happy. Can I have my ice cream now?"

KIDS ARE NATURAL NEGOTIATORS

Have you noticed that kids tend to be keen observers? They observe their surroundings and most importantly they observe you. They observe how you behave. If you are super-duper happy, you might get asked for a lot of favors. If you want your child to stay calm and handle their emotions well, but you always go bananas when something unexpected happens, you are probably demonstrating the wrong model for them.

The main difference between negotiations with your kids and your other negotiations is that your emotions often run high when you deal with your kids. As we've discussed, emotions can run high in your negotiations with adults, too, but the parent–child relationship can intensify emotions like no other situation. This intensity can easily blur your view on what you are trying to achieve for your kids, and with your kids.

Kids have this amazing ability to stay focused on their goals and be persistent in reaching them. My oldest daughter loves watching TV so much that she is always negotiating to get extra TV time. Usually, TV time is at 6 pm for half an hour, but does she wait for TV time to negotiate? No. It could be breakfast time and she is asking for more TV for that evening; it could be 11 pm, when she has just woken up from a nightmare, and she is asking for extra TV for the next day.

It is important to understand that what the kids are doing is not (usually) intended to wear the parents out. Their persistence is their way of being themselves and not giving up until they get what they want.

Kids are natural negotiators; it is our responsibility as parents to keep nurturing this ability while they are growing up. The school environment is made of rules and instructions, assessments, and judgments, so it usually has limited opportunities for kids to negotiate and keep negotiating. The basic skillset that they lose while growing up is to keep asking. As they grow up, they become aware of social expectations and peer pressure, in addition to the rules, and they stop asking. They don't ask the teacher for extra time to complete the assignment. They stop questioning these rules. Or if they do question them, they are not active in challenging them and influencing changes if needed.

DO THEY CARE? DO THEY TRUST YOU?

Kids are looking for caring signals. When I have a heated discussion with my daughter, I tell her that I love her no matter what, and I ask her, "Why would Daddy be naughty here?"

Usually this question helps her understand that there might be another angle to the issue. For instance, why would Daddy bother asking you to wear your raincoat? Daddy might be enjoying his cup of coffee right now instead of bothering you for the fifth time. Would there be another reason apart from annoying you?

Building trust with your kids is crucial.

You're thinking, "What are you telling me here? They are my kids; of course they trust me!" They love you for you—but do they really trust you? Most of the time, we take their trust for granted. Nowadays, it means dropping whatever you are doing and listening to your kids when they want to tell you something. It took several tantrums over a long period to understand that my daughter was thinking I was a bad listener and for her to share this openly with me. In her mind, I was not a good listener and hence not a good person to help solve her problems. Mummy was the go-to person for that.

If you have a big deal coming up with a customer or a boss, would you wait for the night before the meeting to build trust with this person? No; you would be working on building trust through all your interactions with them. The same applies to dealing with your kids.

GOING BANANAS

Am I trying to depict myself as the three-piece-suit super-dad who is always in control of himself and able to manage any child's tantrum all over the world? I can tell you that the reality is far from it, but I keep trying and getting better by the day. I have seen experts in parenting and education lose their composure with their own kids. So relax, no guilt, and keep trying. Even better, share with your kids that you are trying to get better at dealing with them.

Sometimes I lose it and go bananas on small issues with my daughter. This usually happens in the morning when we have only a few minutes to get out the door and my oldest child starts having issues with her clothes or is hungry again. I came to the conclusion that most of the time I am contributing to the drama. The moment I realized that, some changes started to happen. After these distressing situations, I usually sit down with myself, and after clearing the feeling of guilt, I start thinking about what went wrong and how I can change it. Most of the time, a situation escalated because of my own emotions.

(On clearing guilt: I used to call the school in the morning and ask the receptionist to tell my daughter that I love her. After some time, the school sent an email asking parents to stop sending messages to their kids throughout the day. The impetus was either me doing too much of that or other parents going through the same thing. Both options are plausible.)

SHOW, DON'T TELL

If you want your kids to learn how to negotiate better, show them how to do it. Show them how you negotiate with others. It could be as simple as showing them how you get a late checkout at a fully booked hotel. You can lecture them all day on negotiating concepts, but that won't be as effective as their seeing you doing it.

20 | LISTENING TO YOUR KIDS

STORY

Romeo, a four-year-old, was having difficulties before school every morning. He took a long time to put on his clothes, complaining that they were too tight. Then he needed to hop to the toilet five times before getting into the car. On the journey to school, he kept saying that he did not want to go to school. Arriving in front of the school gate, he kissed his daddy goodbye and went inside.

His parents tried initially to talk to him. They kept telling him that his clothes were not tight, that he did not need to go to the toilet five times in three minutes before getting into the car, that school was good, that he seemed to have fun there, and that he was doing well and bringing home some nice projects he did for art, math, or science class.

This approach led nowhere. The same pattern kept going on and on, and his parents got used to it.

A similar pattern occurred every evening. Romeo

would tell his mum that he does not like school. His mum would be in a hurry to go back to her work, and the interaction would go like this: First, she argues with him that school is great and that he will learn great things there. She tells him that he wants to be an inventor when he grows up and school will help him with that. Then she asks him why he doesn't like school. He tells her again that he does not like school, and he keeps repeating this without giving further explanation. Finally, his mum tells him that tomorrow will be fine and then he goes to sleep.

But one evening, after Romeo said again and again that he does not like to go to school, his mum did not react and instead just sat there. Then something happened. Romeo told her that he did not feel well there, and that the kids made fun of him because he talked too much during the games instead of playing. Nobody wanted to play with him during the breaks.

Romeo's parents took him to a therapist, who identified Romeo as a gifted boy with a high IQ. On the playground, while everyone else was having fun in the games, Romeo was overanalyzing every situation, making the games not fun for the other kids. Romeo's parents took him to another school better suited to his needs. Romeo's parents also decided to be more present when they are with him.

DEBRIEF & ADVICE

This story is not about getting your kids to do something like brushing their teeth or doing their homework. This story is about connecting with your kids. What is more powerful in negotiation than creating a bond with the other party? Who deserves most to have a bond with you? This bond is created through listening.

In this story, Romeo's parents were so overwhelmed by his attitude that they forgot to go back to basics and listen. Though we try to listen to our kids, we tend to switch off our attention too quickly, especially with the younger ones. These young kids take time to find their words, and we tend to finish their sentences for them, with the risk of missing the whole story. Or we switch off mentally once they start talking because we can guess what they will say because we have heard it before.

For a couple of years, my daughter kept telling me I was a bad listener. Either I would interrupt her to make my point, or I would guess what she was going to say, only to discover that she was about to tell me something totally different. I am still a work in progress.

When you ask your kids how their day was, and they say it was good, don't move on. Stay silent. Usually they are processing their day, deciding what to tell you and how to tell it. If you move on, you will miss all of that. Train yourself to slow down and pause a lot when dealing with your kids. It helps them have breathing room to catch up on their thoughts and communicate them.

Also, being more present while listening shows your kids that you care about what they say, that you care about them.

21 | SLOWING DOWN TIME

STORY

Ming was on an important video conference when Nora suddenly ran into his home office, shouting, "Daddy, I don't want to eat my dinner!"

Ming asked her gently to leave his office. Nora grew frustrated: "I don't like my dinner; I don't want to eat it."

Ming asked her to go and check with her mummy. Nora told him she is out.

Ming started to get angry. It was his turn to present to the rest of his organization and he was getting distracted. Nora was standing there, waiting for him to offer something else to eat; she was not moving away.

He was about to tell her off. He was in the middle of a very important meeting, and she was disturbing him. He was about to threaten that if she didn't leave his office in 10 seconds, there would be no desert for her for the rest of the week. Yesterday, she ate the same food she's now complaining about, and she was even asking for more. This was all nonsense.

He first calmed himself down, and then said, "Nora, darling, how about you play in your room for 30 minutes? I will come and see you; then we'll go together to check your dinner." Nora accepted and left his office immediately.

When he finished his call, he went to check on her and found her in the kitchen with her nanny. She had already finished her dinner, with the same food she didn't like earlier.

The issue was that she was not hungry before.

DEBRIEF & ADVICE

Ming's first reaction was like what most parents would do when frustrated. We would yell at the kids and talk about our problems ("I am in the middle of a very important call; you need to leave now"). We would expect the kids to be fully understanding and to look at the situation from our perspective. For Nora, though, not wanting the dinner and being asked to eat it was a VERY BIG problem, bigger than Daddy having an important meeting.

What Ming did well was first calming himself down. As mentioned earlier, when we show to kids that we are in control of our emotions, it has double benefits. First, it defuses the tension. Second, it teaches them that managing emotions is doable, since Daddy and Mummy can do it.

Ming thought about threatening. Threats do sometimes work with kids, and issuing threats is often the easiest, fastest way to end a stand-off. Threats are often issued in the heat of the moment, however, and they come with their own set of problems:

1. You are teaching your kids not to discuss, not to negotiate.
2. Kids learn that you don't listen to them.
3. Kids learn by example. Next time I have a bit of power, I will start threatening (watch out when your kids become teenagers).
4. The moment you threaten, your kids shut down and stop listening.

I am not telling you not to put consequences to your kids' actions. I am talking about how to do it. Putting consequences to your kids' actions can be done differently and with a different effect.

When the whole situation is over, Ming can go and see Nora and tell her:

When you came to my room, I was in an important meeting. I got distracted and this made me sad. I was scared not to be able to try my best. I know that you always like to try your best at school. Same for me; I try to do my best at work.

Let's agree on how we can deal with situations like these in the future.

I suggest that when I am in the middle of a meeting and you come over, you do what I ask the first time and trust that I will come and see you as soon as the meeting is over.

Do you agree with that?

Then if you don't listen to me and I need to keep asking you to leave my room, you will not be respecting our deal. In that case, would it be fair that you keep your 15 minutes of TV time for that day, since TV time is a treat for kids who do their homework and are kind to Daddy and Mummy?

We talked about emotions and threats; how about time now? For Nora, the dinner issue was not an issue anymore after half an hour. What Ming did was to stall for time.

How can you stall for time? First, acknowledge the issue. Tell your kids that you realize that their concern is indeed an issue for them. Second, tell them that you want to help them, but you can't do it now, and tell them your reasons. Third, tell them you will come and look at this situation together at a specific time, and offer them something to do in the meantime.

Slowing down time helps parents to regain their

composure and finish whatever they have in hand or in mind. You are of no use to a negotiation with your kids if you are boiling or have lost control of yourself. More importantly for the kids, the additional time will help them calm down. They might determine by themselves whether the issue is a real one of not. If it is not that big of a deal, they will handle it themselves. If it is a big deal, then you will be able to handle it together in a calmer environment.

On the other side, kids are experts at slowing down time. Can I brush my teeth after TV? Can I brush my teeth just before bed? Can I be the last one to brush my teeth?

22 | ROLE-PLAYS TO SEE DIFFERENT PERSPECTIVES

STORY

"What is 16 plus 18?" asked Anna.

"One thousand?" replied the seven-year-old Caroline.

"What!?" said Anna.

"Thirty-six?" said Caroline.

"How do you explain thirty-six?" replied Anna after using all her inner energy to stay calm.

"Because it is a good-quality number, Mummy."

"You are not focused, Caroline. We have been trying to do math for the past half-hour and you are not concentrating."

"I hate doing homework. I don't like you anymore, Mummy. You are very strict; all you do is tell me to do homework!" shouted Caroline.

"I will tell Miss Radish about it tomorrow. She is

going to tell you off, and by the way, no playing with your toys today before going to sleep!" shouted Anna.

Caroline went running to her room and shut her door.

Usually Anna goes running after her to lecture her on the importance of doing homework, saying that if she likes to get good marks at school, she needs to be doing her homework, that it usually takes only 10 minutes, but with Caroline unfocused, it goes always beyond that, that she should not be shouting, that her friends do homework very quickly and then they have enough time to play.

But this time, Anna decided to back off and calm herself down, while also giving Caroline time to calm down. After feeling calm, Anna went to her daughter's room. Caroline was expecting the usual screaming from her mom, but here's what happened instead:

Anna: I understand that you don't like Mummy anymore and that you think I am very strict. Can we play a quick game? Imagine you are Mummy and you have been put in charge of a child for one week. Let's call him Kiko. Kiko does not like to do his homework. Whenever you sit with him, he starts shouting. He starts kicking the chairs. He starts running away. He starts saying that you are awful. What would you do?

Caroline: Does he do that every time, no exception?

Anna: No exception.

Caroline: First, I will lock him in his room. He won't be allowed to come out until he finishes his homework.

Anna: Imagine he keeps screaming from inside his room, and after two hours, he has not done anything.

Caroline: I will tell him that he will not have ice cream for one year. Ha ha!

Anna: Wow, this sounds harsh. You are acting as a super-harsh mummy. Would you like me to say that to you?

Caroline, giggling: No, of course not.

Caroline, after some time thinking: What do you think I should do, Mummy?

DEBRIEF & ADVICE

Kids usually love doing role-plays. Role-playing can be a powerful way to teach kids to look at the other side's perspective while having fun.

Make it a game. "Do you want to pretend to be your sister? Do you want to play your teacher?" Most of the time when asked to role-play, kids realize that what they would do in the situation is more extreme than what you asked them to do.

Also, role-playing helps them feel what the other side

might feel. Role-playing can teach them that in almost every situation, there is usually more than one perspective.

For role-playing to be done successfully, kids need to be in a listening state first. If little Tommy is having a tantrum where he is hating the situation, you bet he won't be open to considering a role-play.

At the end of the role-play, ask the kids what they think and how they feel about the situation.

23 |LET KIDS BE THE BOSS

STORY

Bo was struggling with Alicia, his five-year-old daughter, to brush her hair before school. She never gave him a reason why she did not like it; she just did not want to have her hair brushed. She had a tantrum every morning.

Bo bought three hairbrushes with Alicia's favorite cartoons on them. Alicia was very happy to have these. Bo told her that she is the only one to decide:

1. Who brushes her hair (Daddy or Mummy)
2. Which of the three hairbrushes would be used each day
3. When to brush (before or after breakfast)
4. Which side of the hair to start with

Since then, Alicia has let one of her parents brush her hair every morning.

Chapter 23

DEBRIEF & ADVICE

Initially, Bo was trying to force Alicia to brush her hair. Parents tend to have this hardline position when encountering resistance from their kids: "I am your daddy. I know what's best for you and I am telling you what to do."

When Bo gave Alicia the power to decide the who, when, and how of getting her hair brushed, Alicia felt that her opinion was valued. She was now a key part of the decision process instead of just undergoing this brushing task every day.

Kids want to be in charge most of the time, and they usually want to be *seen* as being in charge as well. They have their own egos; when you take a hardline position with kids, it triggers their egos to push back, just like adults do.

Kids are given instructions to follow all day long at school, at the clubs, at home. Giving them the power to decide can make them feel valued. As a parent, you will increase your chances of getting more things done with them for their own benefit and yours (less tension and drama every day).

You might be thinking, "I can't let my kid be the boss; this is not a proper education." You are right. There are some aspects that are non-negotiable, like ethical values, safety, and health. Letting them be the boss means letting them determine how to implement what matters to you as a parent, rather than letting them decide whether an issue or task matters. In Bo's case, what's necessary and non-negotiable is that Alicia's hair is brushed; what is negotiable and under Alicia's control is how it's done.

You can be transparent with your kids about what you are doing. You can say that such-and-such issue needs to be resolved, but the way it gets resolved is in your hands, and we can sit down and look at options together.

24 | TEACH KIDS HOW TO ASK. YES, ASKING AGAIN

STORY

Mycah was getting ready to leave for school with Adrian, her dad. Swimming was her first class of the day. Just before leaving, she started crying and told her dad that in last week's session, the swimming teacher had taken her out of the intermediate group and put her in the beginner one.

In Mycah's swimming class, the students are divided into three groups: beginner, intermediate, and advanced. Mycah started the year in the advanced group and then got moved to the intermediate one. This was expected as Mycah was a good swimmer but was lacking some skills that the advanced group had. The move to the beginner group was a surprise to her and to her dad. In addition to her swimming class every week at school, Mycah goes to a swimming club every week and her level is between intermediate and advanced.

The first thing that popped into Adrian's mind was, Why on earth Mycah was telling him about this issue only now, 10 minutes before they needed to leave the house? She had a whole week to share this issue with him. This was about to be his first comment, but he thought it wouldn't help.

Adrian then asked Mycah if she had asked the swimming teacher about the reason for this move. She had. The swimming teacher mentioned that in the last session, Mycah was not able to perform some movements required for the intermediate level. Mycah got emotional again, saying that she was really bored at the beginner level and does not want to finish the year in this group. Adrian told Mycah that she needs to talk to her teacher before the lesson starts today. Mycah needs to tell her teacher that she really wants to stay in the intermediate group and that she did not perform well in the last session because she was distracted. Mycah could share that she feels very bored and is not learning much in the beginner group, and ask her teacher what she needs to do to stay in the intermediate group.

Mycah was very hesitant to ask her teacher, who was known to be very tough. Adrian insisted that the only way for Mycah to try getting what she wanted was to ask. Adrian usually reminds Mycah to think about the worst-case scenario. In this case, the teacher would keep her in the beginner class, where she was already, so there was nothing to lose if she asked.

When Adrian picked up Mycah from school at the end of the day, she was beaming with joy. She was back in the intermediate group.

DEBRIEF & ADVICE

It turned out that Mycah not only asked to go back to the intermediate group, but also did it in a very tactful way.

She went to her teacher before the lesson started. She told her that she was feeling sad to be back at the beginner level, that she felt bored, and that she had not tried her best in the last session. She asked the teacher to let her participate at the intermediate level for today's lesson, and said that if she did not perform all the required movements, it would be fair for her to switch to the beginner level. The teacher told her she was okay with that.

During the lesson, Mycah performed all the required movements, so she was able to stay in the intermediate group. If she had not asked, the teacher would have kept her in the beginner group for the rest of the school term.

Encourage your kids to get comfortable with asking for what they want. They might be comfortable with asking you. Are they comfortable doing that with their teachers, with their uncles and aunties, with their sports coaches, with their friends?

Let your kids consider the downside of asking, which is usually nonexistent. Ask them to think about the downside of not asking, which is not getting what matters to them. Most of the downside of asking is in our heads. We limit ourselves by coming up with all the reasons that asking will be harmful for such-and-such a situation. Why is that? Because asking is uncomfortable, and our reptilian brain does not like discomfort and will come up with all the possible excuses for not taking action.

Beyond getting comfortable with asking, kids also need to learn how to ask.

Kids might get annoying when asking, sounding like a broken record with a sense of entitlement: "Mummy, can I play in the garden? Mummy, I would like to play in the garden. Mummy, please please please, I am craving to play in the garden. Pleaaaaaaaaaaaaaaase, Mummmmmmmmmmmy." Virtually raise your hand if any of this sounds familiar.

Instead of letting them repeat themselves endlessly, encourage them to justify their requests and to tell the other person how they are feeling. They can also start with a smaller request to build up to the bigger one they are after.

Mycah did all of that very well. First, she explained her request and shared how she was feeling; then she left the decision to the teacher. She did not challenge her teacher's authority. She did not tell her teacher that she made a big mistake by bringing her back to the beginner group. She did not try to force her teacher to accept her request. She asked for something small: to have a chance to try again today. This made it easy for the teacher to say yes.

Instead of reminding kids that if they don't ask, they don't get, I advise reminding them that if they don't ask well, they don't get.

Encourage your kids to be bold and ask for what matters to them. Tell them there is always a tomorrow, and every win gained today builds a foundation for a new win for tomorrow.

RECOMMENDED READING

I hope you enjoyed reading this book. Capturing all concepts, techniques, and frameworks of negotiation in one single book is not possible. Here is a non-exhaustive list of books on negotiation written by experts in history, business deal making, and psychology. You can find so many perspectives about negotiation in these books and pick up the ideas that resonate with you.

- Alexandra Carter, *Ask for More: 10 Questions to Negotiate Anything*
- Christopher Hadnagy, *Human Hacking: Win Friends, Influence People, and Leave Them Better Off for Having Met You*
- Daniel Shapiro and Roger Fisher, *Building Agreement: Using Emotions as You Negotiate*
- Deepak Malhotra, *Negotiating the Impossible: How to Break Deadlocks and Resolve Ugly Conflicts (without Money or Muscle)*
- Francis Walder, *The Negotiator: The Masterclass at Saint-Germain*

- Herb Cohen, *You Can Negotiate Anything: The World's Best Negotiator Tells You How to Get What You Want*
- Joe Navarro, *What Every BODY Is Saying: An Ex-FBI Agent's Guide to Speed-Reading People*
- Kate Murphy, *You're Not Listening: What You're Missing and Why It Matters*
- Laurent Combalbert & Marwan Mery, Negotiator: *The Reference for all Negotiation*
- Mo Gawdat, *That Little Voice In Your Head: Adjust the Code That Runs Your Brain*
- Robert B. Cialdini, *Pre-Suasion: A Revolutionary Way to Influence and Persuade*
- Stuart Diamond, *Getting More: How You Can Negotiate to Succeed in Work and Life*
- William Ury, *Getting to Yes with Yourself (and Other Worthy Opponents)*

ACKNOWLEDGEMENTS

Writing this book would not have been possible without the unwavering support and inspiration of numerous individuals who have played a significant role in my journey. To each of you, I extend my deepest gratitude and appreciation.

- My parents, who instilled in me the belief that negotiation opens doors and creates opportunities.
- My wife, who has been my continuous support. She showed me that to influence others effectively, I must first influence myself.
- Catherine E. Oliver, my editor. Her sharp eye for detail and her ability to find gaps in my work have helped immensely to shape this book.
- Herb Cohen and Stuart Diamond. Years ago, their works were my first encounter with the world of professional negotiation.
- To all the individuals I've had the privilege to negotiate with and coach over the years, I owe you a debt of gratitude. I have learned something valuable from each one of you.

ABOUT THE AUTHOR

Anis Bennani works as head of infrastructure acquisition at one of the big tech companies. He has spent over a decade in deal making in the technology field, on both the buying and sales sides, across multiple countries and regions. He has been directly managing or coaching negotiators in high-stakes, multimillion-dollar negotiations. He is passionate about coaching and helping others to get what matters to them.

MESSAGE FROM THE AUTHOR

Dear reader,

Many thanks for your interest in the book.

I would love to hear your feedback. You can email me at *anis.bennani@gettingwhatmatters.com*. I will try to respond to each email.

If you enjoyed reading the book, I hope you will consider sharing this. Here are some suggestions:

- Amazon reviews—I will be grateful if you can take a few minutes to rate and review the book.
- Social media, especially LinkedIn—You can post and tell your network about the book. Feel free to tag me: *https://www.linkedin.com/in/anisbennani/*

All the best for getting what matters to you.

Anis Bennani

Printed in Great Britain
by Amazon

44692735R00086